CIVIL WAR FILMS FOR TEACHERS AND HISTORIANS

William B. Russell III

University Press of America,® Inc.
Lanham · Boulder · New York · Toronto · Plymouth, UK

Copyright © 2008 by
University Press of America,® Inc.
4501 Forbes Boulevard
Suite 200
Lanham, Maryland 20706
UPA Acquisitions Department (301) 459-3366

Estover Road
Plymouth PL6 7PY
United Kingdom

All rights reserved
Printed in the United States of America
British Library Cataloging in Publication Information Available

Library of Congress Control Number: 2007936087
ISBN-13: 978-0-7618-3914-9 (paperback : alk. paper)
ISBN-10: 0-7618-3914-3 (paperback : alk. paper)

∞™ The paper used in this publication meets the minimum
requirements of American National Standard for Information
Sciences—Permanence of Paper for Printed Library Materials,
ANSI Z39.48—1984

CONTENTS

List of Tables	vii
Preface & Overview	ix
Acknowledgments	xi
Chapter One, "Introduction"	1
Civil War on Film	1
Using Civil War Films in the Classroom	2
Chapter Two, "Teaching with Film"	5
The Russell Model for Using Film	5
Legal Issues	11
Chapter Three, "Filmography"	15
Abe Lincoln in Illinois	16
Abraham Lincoln	16
Alvarez Kelly	17
Andersonville	17
Andersonville Trial, The	17
Arizona Bushwhackers, The	18
Arizona Kid, The	18
Autobiography of Miss Jane Pittman, The	19
Band of Angels	19
Battle, The	19
Beguiled, The	20
Beulah Land	20
Birth of a Nation, The	21
Blood and Honor	21
Blue and the Gray, The	21
Calvary Charge	22

Charlotte Forten's Mission: Experiment in Freedom	22
Civil War Diary	23
Class of '61	23
Cold Mountain	23
Dances with Wolves	24
Dark Commander	24
Day Lincoln was Shot, The	25
Drummer of the 8th, The	25
Drums in the Deep South	25
Escape from Fort Bravo	26
Fastest Guitar Player Alive, The	26
Friendly Persuasion	27
Fugitive, The	27
Gangs of New York	28
General, The	28
General Spanky	28
Gettysburg	29
Glory	29
Gods and Generals	30
Gone With the Wind	30
Good, the Bad, and the Ugly, The	30
Granddad	31
Great Locomotive Chase, The	31
Guns of Fort Petticoat	32
Hangman's Knot	32
His Trust	33
His Trust Fulfilled	33
Horses Soldier, The	34
House with Closed Shutters, The	34
How the West Was Won	35
Hunley, The	35
In the Border States	35
Ironclads	36
Jezebel	36
Journey to Shiloh	37
Last Samurai, The	37
Lincoln	38

Contents

Little Colonel, The	38
Little Women	38
Littlest Rebel, The	39
Love Me Tender	39
Macho Callahan	40
Major Dundee	40
Man from Colorado, The	41
Mosby's Marauders	41
North and South	41
North and South, Book II	42
North and South, Book III	42
Occurrence at Owl Creek Bridge, An	43
Of Human Hearts	43
Oldest Living Confederate Widow Tells All, The	43
Outlaw Josey Wales, The	44
Pharaoh's Army	44
Private History of a Campaign that Failed, The	45
Proud Rebel, The	45
Raintree County	46
Red Badge of Courage, The	46
Ride with the Devil	47
Rio Lobo	47
Roots	48
Rose and the Jackal, The	48
Santa Fe Trail	49
Seven Angry Men	49
Shenandoah	49
So the Red Rose	50
South of St. Louis	50
Southern Yankee, A	50
Springfield Rifle	51
Swords and Hearts	51
Tennessee Johnson	52
Their One Love	52
They Died with Their Boots On	53
Undefeated, The	53
Virginia City	54
Wicked Spring	54

Young Mr. Lincoln	55
Chapter Four, "Interview with James McPherson"	57
Appendix A	61
References	65
Index	67

LIST OF TABLES

Table 1.1, *Russell Model for Using Film*   7

PREFACE & OVERVIEW

This book was written to provide teachers and historians with a filmography of Civil War films. This book will provide teachers and historians with nearly one-hundred movies that pertain to the Civil War, as well as guidelines for using film in the classroom. Using film as an enhancement tool is very effective and has been found to have many positive outcomes on student learning and interest. However, for film to be effective it must be used appropriately. This book provides a research based model, the *Russell Model for Using Film*, for using film appropriately in the classroom.

Chapter one, "Introduction," will provide readers with a brief historical account of the Civil War on film and a foundation for using Civil War films in the classroom.

Chapter two, "Teaching with Film," will provide readers with a research based model, the *Russell Model for Using Film*, for using film appropriately in the classroom. This four stage model will help ensure appropriate film use. As well, chapter two will discuss the legal issues surrounding film use in the classroom. Specifically, the United States Code on Copyright, the Fair Use policy, and the Recording of Off-Air Broadcasting.

Chapter three, "Filmography," will provide readers with the Civil War Filmography (A-Z). This chapter includes nearly one-hundred movies that pertain to the Civil War. The filmography does not include every Civil War film ever made, but is does include the large majority of Hollywood films (with sound) and a small selection of films from the silent film era. The films were selected in large part based on availability. The movies are listed in alphabetical order and each movie listed in the filmography includes the following: title, year, rating, director, producer, runtime, country/language, color, company, distributor, and a summary when available.

Chapter four, "Interview with James McPherson," provides readers with insight into the mind of Pulitzer Prize winning author James McPherson. This chapter is an interview with James McPherson that I had with him in April of 2007.

Remember, when used appropriately, film is a powerful and visually stimulating tool. However, film must be used to enhance the lesson, not as the lesson.

William B Russell III, Ph.D.
University of Central Florida, August 2007

ACKNOWLEGMENTS

I would like to express a sincere thank you to my family and friends.

A special thank you goes to James McPherson, The Internet Movie Database (http://www.imdb.com), the Motion Picture Association of America (MPAA), and to University Press of America.

I would also like to thank, my former graduate assistant Austen Johnson and my former Civil War professor, Jim Jones of Florida State University.

ONE

INTRODUCTION

Civil War on Film

Since the Civil War, its events have been reproduced through various mediums. After the war, writers published articles, stories, and books pertaining to the Civil War. Printed works that dealt with the Civil War were popular among readers. Based on the publishing success of Civil War material, playwrights followed suit, hoping to have the same success. However, stage plays about the Civil War were not received well. Stage plays pertaining to the Civil War did not become popular until a romantic story was woven into the storyline (Chadwick, 2001).

George Eastman, the founder of Kodak, created flexible celluloid in 1888/9, which was the basis for motion picture film. Then, in 1891, Thomas Edison introduced the kinetoscope, a small peephole viewer for watching short and simple motion pictures. Eastman's creation of celluloid and Edison's kinetoscope helped spawn an era of silent films. Silent films were the only available films in the early 1900's, and it was not until 1929/30 that films with sound became readily available.

With the creation of film, movie directors naturally followed the stage plays, hoping for the same success. The silent movie era bombarded the United States of America. By 1910, there were ten thousand movie theaters in the United States (Chadwick, 2001).

The first Civil War-era film created was the 1903 version of *Uncle Tom's Cabin*. In 1908, the first true Civil War battle movie was created, *Days of '61*. These films started a Civil War movement that impacted the rest of the world. In 1907, thirteen civil war movies were made, in 1909 twenty-three were made, in 1910 thirty-four were made, and about one hundred Civil War movies were made per year until 1916 (Chadwick, 2001 & Spehr, 1961). As well, it is estimated that since the silent film era, there have been nearly two hundred full length movies created that pertain to the Civil War (Chadwick, 2001).

Using Film in the Classroom

Using film in the classroom is an effective strategy (Paris, 1997). Film has been shown to help develop students' historical understanding (Allen, 2005) by providing visual images of historical events.

Historians have found that film images impact and influence a person's perspective of history (O'Connor & Jackson, 1988). Furthermore, historians have also found that history on film can be an accurate interpretation of history (Rosenstone, 1995) and that film can bring students closer to the people and events that they are studying (Matz & Pingatore, 2005).

Film is an enhancement tool for the curriculum, it is not the curriculum, and so by using film as a tool, teachers allow students to take ownership in learning. By taking an element (film) that has real life application and incorporating it into the curriculum students will have higher levels of interest in the lesson.

Using authentic activities in the classroom help to achieve instructional goals like retention, understanding, reasoning, and critical thinking (Driscoll, 2005). Allen (2005) explains that examining films can promote historical thinking and awareness of historical prospective.

Engle (1960; 2003) stressed decision-making as the heart of social studies education. Pressing that students learn the decision making process, instead of content memorization. Film can help provoke meaningful inquiry of a historical event, thus allowing students to make insightful decisions based on what they viewed and what the teacher does to support the curriculum.

According to Allen (2005) using film in the classroom can help students develop historical thinking skills. However, if teachers fail to use film appropriately, the ability to help students develop historical thinking skills will be lost. Historical thinking skills are extremely important, so important that in 1994, The National Center for History in Schools (NCHS) developed five standards for historical thinking:
1) Chronological Thinking
2) Historical Comprehension
3) Historical Analysis and Interpretation
4) Historical Research Capabilities
5) Historical Issues-Analysis and Decision-Making

However, for film to be effective it must be used appropriately. Appropriate film use will be discussed in Chapter Two, "Teaching with Film."

Note
*Sections and/or parts of this chapter were reprinted from Russell, W. (2007). Using film in the social studies. Lanham, MD: University Press of America Inc. with written permission.

TWO

TEACHING WITH FILM

As discussed in the previous chapter, teaching with film can be an effective teaching strategy. However, teaching with film can also be seen as a waste of precious instructional time (Reform K-12, 2006). Reform K-12 is an online chat room by which teachers, parents, administrators, and others discuss varying educational issues. One complaint described an irate parent whose child had viewed over sixty-seven Hollywood movies in a special education classroom from August to November (four months) of a single school year. Another complaint describes how schools have used films as non-instructional time, allowing Fridays to become "Movie Friday" (Reform K-12, 2006). These concerns are genuine and are serious setbacks for teachers who use film in the classroom, because it gives teaching with film a negative image. Allen (2005) & Russell (2007), explain that for film to be effective it must be used appropriately and not misused or abused.

The Russell Model for Using Film

The *Russell Model for Using Film* is a four-stage model for using film in the classroom. Many teachers use film and think they use it effectively, but they do not follow the research-based guidelines for using film as laid out in the *Russell Model for Using Film* (see Table 1.1).

Russell Model for Using Film
1. The Preparation Stage
2. The Pre-Viewing Stage
3. Watching the Film Stage
4. The Culminating Activity Stage

Many of the activities that are found in the *Russell Model for Using Film* have been found to help increase student achievement. Allen (1955) found that if teachers announce a test during the pre-viewing stage that students will learn more than students who were unaware of the test prior to showing the film. Allen also found that if teachers introduce and prepare the class for a film during the pre-viewing stage, students retained more content information then students who did not receive the same introduction and preparation.

By using the *Russell Model for Using Film*, teachers will help ensure that film is used to enhance the curriculum, not as the curriculum. Furthermore, teachers will help ensure that film is used appropriately and legally. The *Russell Model for Using Film* should be used as a guide; however teachers still need to make sure that all professional, ethical, and legal standards are being upheld.

Table 1.1 *Russell Model for Using Film*

Stage 1: The Preparation Stage

The preparation stage is the most important stage of the *Russell Model for Using Film*.
This is the planning stage of the model. The preparation stage includes the following, but is not limited to the following:
(* Denotes required activities)

- Create lesson plans that incorporate film, while still meeting instructional goals/objectives, state standards, national standards, and that adheres to all legal requirements *
- Preview the film! Instructors must preview all films before using a film in the classroom *
- Create a specific pre-viewing activity (see stage 2)*
- Create a specific watching the film activity (see stage 3)
- Create a specific culminating activity related to the film (see stage 4) *
- Get permission from administration to use the film in the classroom *
- Get permission from students' parents/guardians that permit viewing *
- Arrange for appropriate equipment (DVD/VCR Player, LCD projector, TV, etc...) *
- Arrange classroom for viewing *

Remember:
Film should <u>NOT</u> be used as a time-filler. Film should <u>NOT</u> be used as the lesson, but only to enhance the lesson.

Table 1.1 (Continued) *Russell Model for Using Film*

Stage 2: The Pre-viewing Stage

The pre-viewing stage is done prior to students viewing the film.
The pre-viewing stage includes the following, but is not limited to the following: (* Denotes required activities)

- Introduction of the film to students *
- Explain the purpose for viewing the film *
- Introduction of new vocabulary *
- Relate the film to student's prior knowledge *
- Relate the film to student's everyday lives *
- Relate the film to other content areas *
- Clarify any cinematic terminology (e.g. close-up, voice-over) *
- Discuss what is required during the viewing of the film *
- Discuss the culminating activity that will follow the viewing of the film *
- Discuss the background of the film *
- Collect permission slips from parents/guardians (Ideally, this should be done days prior to showing the film. Furthermore, administrative permission should be obtained prior to obtaining parent/guardian permission) *

Other Ideas for the Pre-viewing Stage
- K-W-L: What I Know, What I Want to Know, and What I Learned
- Read film reviews
- Read interviews with the star, director, producer, etc....

Table 1.1 (Continued) *Russell Model for Using Film*

Stage 3: Watching the Film Stage

Watching the film stage is where students actually view the film. The watching the film stage includes the following: (* Denotes required activities)

- Watch the film*

Showing the entire film is appropriate when necessary, as is showing small segments or clips. Research has been shown to support both types of film use. Stopping the film occasionally to highlight an important point, concept, issue, and/or scene is appropriate.

Other Ideas for Watching the Film Stage

- Have students take notes (If notes are required, the teacher must provide ample light and time for writing the notes)
- Complete a guided activity (Some films have pre-made guided activities)
- Answer questions created by the teacher

Table 1.1 (Continued) *Russell Model for Using Film*

Stage 4: The Culminating Activity Stage

The culminating activity stage is done after students have watched the film.
The culminating activity stage includes the following, but is not limited to the following: (* Denotes required activities)

- Stop the film*
- Review and discuss major points, concepts, issues, and/or scenes*
- Assess student learning (see assessment ideas below)*

Assessment Ideas

- Class discussion
- Class debate
- Rewrite the ending of the film
- Write a review of the film
- Take a test/quiz
- Complete a worksheet
- Reenactment (Have students reenact a scene from the film)
- Mock interview with the star, director, and/or producer of the film
- Have students analyze and evaluate the film

Legal Issues

Many teachers use film, however they are unaware of the legal issues surrounding its use. It is extremely crucial that teachers understand and follow the law, when using copyrighted materials. The two main legal issues surrounding film use in the classroom are 1) school/school district policies and regulations and 2) copyright.

School/school district policies and regulations should be upheld. Since policies and regulations change from school to school and district to district, teachers need to check with school administrators or school district administrators to obtain the policies and regulations for using film in the classroom.

As stated above, policies and regulations for using film in the classroom change from school to school and district to district. A basic policy for using film in the classroom will be similar to the following:

1) All films must be used in the classroom for instructional purposes.
2) Films with a rating of "G" may be used for instructional purposes with teacher approval and administrative permission.
3) Films with a rating of "PG" may be used for instructional purposes with teacher approval, administrative permission, and parent/guardian permission.
4) Films with a rating of "PG-13" may be used for instructional purposes with teacher approval, administrative permission, and parent/guardian permission.
5) Films with a rating of "R" and/or higher cannot be shown (See Appendix A for explanation of film ratings).

Copyright laws are federal and are established by the United States Copyright Office. Section 110 (1) of Title 17 of the United States Code on Copyright and Conditions cites the following exemption for the use of copyrighted films for educational purposes:

> Performance or display of a work by instructors or pupils in the course of face-to-face teaching activities of a nonprofit

educational institution, in a classroom or similar place devoted to instruction, unless in the case of a motion picture or other audiovisual work, the performance, or the display of individual images, is given by means of a copy that was not lawfully made under this title, and that the person responsible for the performance knew or had reason to believe was not lawfully made (ww.copyright.gov/title17/92chap1.html#110).

Simply put, a film must be used in a non-profit educational institution, in an instructional class that is meeting face-to-face, and for educational purposes, not entertainment or recreation. As well, educators can use a film that has been rented at a video store, borrowed from a library, and/or purchased, as long as the above regulations are adhered to.

However, teachers should not make copies of films, use films as public performance, and/or make a profit from showing films. Teachers can make copies of public television programs for educational use in the classroom. This practice is covered under the fair use code of copyrighted material. What is fair use? Section 107 of Title 17 (1) of the United States Code on Copyright and Conditions explains the fair use guidelines for the use of copyrighted materials for educational purposes:

Notwithstanding the provisions of sections 106 and 106A, the fair use of a copyrighted work, including such use by reproduction in copies or phonorecords or by any other means specified by that section, for purposes such as criticism, comment, news reporting, teaching (including multiple copies for classroom use), scholarship, or research, is not an infringement of copyright. In determining whether the use made of a work in any particular case is a fair use the factors to be considered shall include—

1) the purpose and character of the use, including whether such use is of a commercial nature or is for nonprofit educational purposes;
2) the nature of the copyrighted work;

3) the amount and substantiality of the portion used in relation to the copyrighted work as a whole; and
4) the effect of the use upon the potential market for or value of the copyrighted work (www.copyright.gov/title17/92chap1.html#107).

The complete United States Code on Copyright and Conditions can be accessed via the Internet. The web address is http://www.copyright.gov/title17/.

Furthermore, to qualify as fair use, the Federal Guidelines for Off-Air Recording of Broadcast Programming for Educational Purposes (1981) should be adhered to. Those guidelines are as follows:

1) The guidelines were developed to apply only to off-air recording by nonprofit educational institutions.
2) A broadcast program may be recorded off-air simultaneously with broadcast transmission -- (including simultaneous cable re-transmission) and retained by a nonprofit educational institution for a period not to exceed the first forty-five (45) consecutive calendar days after date of recording. Upon conclusion of such retention period, all off-air recordings must be ceased or destroyed immediately. "Broadcast programs" are television programs transmitted by television stations for reception by the general public without charge.
3) Off-air recordings may be used by individual teachers in the course of relevant teaching activities, and repeated once only when instructional reinforcement is necessary, in classrooms and similar places devoted to instruction within a single buildings, cluster, or campus, as well as in the homes of students receiving formalized home instruction, during the first ten (10) consecutive school days in the forty-five (45) day calendar day retention period. "School days" are school session days-- not counting weekends, holidays, vacations, examina-

tion periods, or other scheduled interruptions--within the forty-five (45) calendar day retention period.

4) Off-Air recordings may be made only at the request of and used by individual teachers, and may not be regularly recorded in anticipation of requests. No broadcast program may be recorded off-air more than once at the request of the same teacher, regardless of the number of times the program may be broadcast.

5) A limited number of copies may be reproduced from each off-air recording to meet the legitimate needs of teachers under these guidelines. Each such additional copy shall be subject to all provisions governing the original recording.

6) After the first ten (10) consecutive school days, off-air recordings may be used up to the end of the forty-five (45) calendar day retention period only for teacher evaluation purposes, i.e., to determine whether or not to include the broadcast program in the teaching curriculum, and may not be used in the recording institution for student exhibition or any other non-evaluation purpose without authorization.

7) Off-air recordings need not be used in their entirety, but the recorded programs may not be altered from their original content. Off-air recordings may not be physically or electronically combined or merged to constitute teaching anthologies or compilations.

8) All copies of off-air recordings must include the copyright notice on the broadcast programs as recorded.

9) Educational Institutions are expected to establish the appropriate control procedures to maintain the integrity of these guidelines (p. E4750-E4752).

Note

*Sections and/or parts of this chapter were reprinted from Russell, W. (2007). *Using film in the social studies*. Lanham, MD: University Press of America Inc. with written permission.

THREE

FILMOGRAPHY

What is a filmography? A filmography is simply a list of movies pertaining to a particular category. This filmography is a list of available movies pertaining to the Civil War era. This filmography does not include every Civil War film ever made, but it does include the large majority of Hollywood films (with sound) and a small selection of films from the silent film era. The films included were selected in large part based on availability and are not considered superior to any other film not included. The majority of the films can found at a local video rental store or can be purchased from an online store (e.g. www.amazon.com) for a nominal price.

According to Chadwick (2001) there are over five hundred Civil War films from the silent film era, however only a small number are available for viewing. Since the large majority of these films are not available for viewing, only available films have been included in this filmography.

Furthermore, documentaries, home movies, government films, and education films have been excluded from the filmography. However, one cannot discuss the Civil War on film with out including Ken Burns' *The Civil War* (1990). This documentary is a marvelous creation and is an excellent resource for anyone interested in the Civil War.

This filmography contains nearly one hundred movies that deal with some aspect of Civil War. The movies are listed in alphabetical order and each movie listed in the filmography includes the following: year, rating, director, producer, runtime, country/language, color, company, distributor, and a summary when available.

A

Abe Lincoln in Illinois (1940) NR (Not Rated)
AKA: *Spirit of the People*
Director: John Cromwell
Producer: Max Gordon
Runtime: 110 Minutes
Country/Language: USA/English
Color: Black and White
Company: Max Gordon Plays & Pictures Corporation
Distributor: Turner Home Video

This film covers the period from Lincoln's early years as a Kentucky woodsman until his election to the Presidency in 1860. Included are his first love, his marriage, the Illinois law practice and his debates with Stephen Douglas.

Abraham Lincoln (1930) NR
AKA: *D.W. Griffith's 'Abraham Lincoln'*
Director: D.W. Griffith
Producer: D.W. Griffith
Runtime: 97 Minutes
Country/Language: USA/English
Color: Black and White
Company: D.W. Griffith Productions
Distributor: Reel Media International

A collection of brief vignettes about Lincoln's early life include his birth, early jobs, (unsubstantiated) affair with Ann Rutledge, courtship of Mary Todd, and the Lincoln-Douglas debates; his presidency and the Civil War are followed in somewhat more detail, though without actual battle scenes; film concludes with the assassination.

***Alvarez Kelly* (1970) NR**
Director: Edward Dmytryk
Producer: Ray David
Runtime: 110 Minutes
Country/Language: USA/English
Color: Color
Company: Columbia Pictures Corporation
Distributor: Columbia Tri-Star Home Video

A suave Mexican cattleman Alvarez Kelly has little interest in the Civil War except to make some money. But after a long drive to deliver cattle to the Unionists he finds himself kidnapped by Confederate Colonel Tom Rossiter. With his hungry troops surrounded in Richmond the Colonel intends, one way or the other, to persuade Kelly to help steal the herd and move it into town.

***Andersonville* (1996) NR**
Director: John Frankenheimer
Producer: John Frankenheimer
Runtime: 166 Minutes
Country/Language: USA/English
Color: Color
Company: Turner Pictures
Distributor: Warner Home Video

A Civil War version of *Schindler's List* looks at the atrocities that occurred in the 1864 prisoner-of-war camp run by the Confederacy in Georgia. The prison originally planned to house 8,000, eventually swelled to 33,000 which left little shelter, food or water for the prisoners and unclean conditions.

***Andersonville Trial, The* (1970) NR**
Director: George Scott
Producer: Lewis Freedman

Runtime: 150 Minutes
Country/Language: USA/English
Color: Color
Company: N/A
Distributor: Public Broadcasting Service

A dramatization of the 1865 war-crimes trial of Henry Wirz, commandant of the notorious Confederate POW camp at Andersonville, Georgia.

Arizona Bushwhackers, The (1968) NR
Director: Lesley Selander
Producer: A.C. Lyles
Runtime: 87 Minutes
Country/Language: USA/English
Color: Color
Company: A.C. Lyles Productions
Distributor: Paramount Pictures

During the Civil War, a Confederate spy takes a job as marshal of a small western town as a cover for his espionage activities. However, he soon finds out that a local businessman is selling weapons to a band of rampaging Indians.

Arizona Kid, The (1939) NR
Director: Joseph Kane
Producer: Joseph Kane
Runtime: 61 Minutes
Country/Language: USA/English
Color: Black and White
Company: Republic Pictures
Distributor: Reel Media International

Roy is a Confederate officer stationed in Missouri during the Civil War. He must put an end to outlaw gangs working under the pretense of service to the Confederacy.

Autobiography of Miss Jane Pittman, The **(1974) NR**
Director: John Korty
Producer: Philip Barry Jr.
Runtime: 110 Minutes
Country/Language: USA/English
Color: Color
Company: Tomorrow Entertainment
Distributor: CBS Television

In February 1962, as the civil rights movement reaches Bayonne, Louisiana, a New York journalist arrives to interview Jane Pitman, who has just turned 110. She tells him her story dating back to her earliest memories before slavery ended. A long walk toward freedom, marriage to Joe Pitman, her adopted son Ned's work as an educator, helping to raise Jimmy (who returns as a civil rights worker) and her own decision to become involved in contemporary issues. In between the chapters of her life, the present-day struggles of blacks in Bayonne, urged on by Jimmy, are dramatized.

B

Band of Angels **(1957) NR**
Director: Raoul Walsh
Producer: Raoul Walsh
Runtime: 125 Minutes
Country/Language: USA/English
Color: Color
Company: Warner Bros. Pictures
Distributor: Warner Bros. Pictures

Summary Not Available

Battle, The **(1911) NR**
Director: D.W. Griffith
Producer: D.W. Griffith

Runtime: 19 Minutes
Country/Language: USA/English
Color: Black and White
Company: Biograph Company
Distributor: Kino Video

Union soldiers march off to battle amid cheering crowds. After the battle turns against the Union Army, one soldier runs away, hiding in his girlfriend's house. Ashamed of his cowardice, he finds his courage and crosses enemy lines to bring help to his trapped comrades.

***Beguiled, The* (1971) R**
Director: Don Siegel
Producer: Don Siegel
Runtime: 105 Minutes
Country/Language: USA/English
Color: Color
Company: Jennings Lang
Distributor: Universal Pictures

During the civil war, injured Yankee soldier, John McBurney is rescued on the verge of death by a teenage girl from a southern boarding school. She manages to get him back to the school and at first the all-female staff and pupils are scared. As he starts to recover, one by one he charms them and the atmosphere becomes filled with jealousy and deceit.

***Beulah Land* (1980) NR**
Director: Harry Falk & Virgil W. Vogel
Producer: David Gerber
Runtime: 120 Minutes
Country/Language: USA/English
Color: Color
Company: Columbia Pictures Television
Distributor: Columbia Pictures Television

This sweeping epic dramatized the lives of two Georgia families during the early-to-mid 1800s: the Kendricks, who resided on the Beulah Land plantation, and the Davises, who owned the Oaks plantation. Both families loved, prospered and lost during this period, and were both touched by the events of the Civil War.

Birth of a Nation, The **(1915) NR**
AKA: *Clansman, The*
Director: D.W. Griffith
Producer: D.W. Griffith
Runtime: 187 Minutes
Country/Language: USA/English
Color: Black and White
Company: D.W. Griffith Corporation
Distributor: Reel Media International

Two brothers, Phil and Ted Stoneman, visit their friends (the Cameron family) in Piedmont, South Carolina. This friendship is affected by the Civil War, as the Stoneman's and the Cameron's must join up opposite armies. The consequences of the War in their lives are shown in connection to major historical events, like the development of the Civil War itself, Lincoln's assassination, and the birth of the Ku Klux Klan.

Blood and Honor **(2000) NR**
AKA: *Battle for Glory*
Director: Donald Farmer
Producer: Maurice Fagan
Runtime: N/A
Country/Language: USA/English
Color: Color
Company: Crusade Productions
Distributor: Wisdom Entertainment

Summary Not Available

Blue and the Gray, The **(1982) NR**
Director: Andrew McLaglen

Producer: Larry White
Runtime: 378 Minutes
Country/Language: USA/English
Color: Color
Company: Columbia Pictures Television
Distributor: RCA/Columbia Pictures Home Video

The film depicts America just before and during the Civil War, as seen through the eyes of an artist correspondent.

C

Calvary Charge (1951) NR
AKA: *Last Outpost, The*
Director: Lewis Foster
Producer: William Pine
Runtime: 89 Minutes
Country/Language: USA/English
Color: Color
Company: Pine-Thomas Productions
Distributor: Ivy Classics

Two brothers who are not the best friends because they were fighting on different sides during the Civil War have to cooperate in order to defend themselves against an attack of Indians.

Charlotte Forten's Mission: Experiment in Freedom (1985) NR
AKA: *Half-Slave, Half-Free 2*
Director: Barry Crane
Producer: N/A
Runtime: 125 Minutes
Country/Language: USA/English
Color: Color
Company: N/A
Distributor: Public Broadcasting Service (PBS)

The film is a drama based on the true story of Charlotte Forten, a young black woman who became an integral part of President

Lincoln's 'great experiment.' During the Civil War, Southern troops were forced off the Sea Islands (off the coast of Georgia), which left 8,000 slaves free. Miss Forten's mission was to journey south to Sea Island and lead those slaves in the transition from slavery to freedom, where she sought to give newly freed black children a decent education and chance for a better life.

***Civil War Diary* (1990) NR**
AKA: *Across Five Aprils*
Director: Kevin Meyer
Producer: Robert C. Peters
Runtime: 82 Minutes
Country/Language: USA/English
Color: Color
Company: N/A
Distributor: Rhine Video

Summary Not Available

***Class of '61* (1993) NR**
Director: Gregory Hoblit
Producer: Steven Spielberg
Runtime: N/A
Country/Language: USA/English
Color: Color
Company: Amblin Entertainment
Distributor: MCA/Universal Home Video

Summary Not Available

***Cold Mountain* (2003) R**
Director: Anthony Minghella
Producer: Bob and Harvey Weinstein
Runtime: 155 Minutes
Country/Language: USA/English
Color: Color
Company: Miramax
Distributor: Miramax

Cold Mountain tells the story of a wounded Confederate soldier named Inman who struggles on a perilous journey to get back home to Cold Mountain, N.C. as well as to Ada, the woman he left behind before going off to fight in the Civil War. Along the way, he meets a long line of interesting and colorful characters, while back at home, Ada is learning the ropes of managing her deceased father's farm with Ruby, a scrappy drifter who assists and teaches Ada along the way.

D

Dances With Wolves **(1990) PG-13**
Director: Kevin Costner
Producer: Kevin Costner
Runtime: 236 Minutes
Country/Language: USA/English
Color: Color
Company: Tig Productions
Distributor: MGM/UA Home Entertainment Inc.

Lt. John Dunbar is dubbed a hero after he accidentally leads Union troops to a victory during the Civil War. He requests a position on the western frontier, but finds it deserted. He soon finds out he is not alone. He meets a wolf he dubs "two-socks" and a curious Indian tribe. Dunbar quickly makes friends with the tribe, and discovers a white woman who was raised by the Indians. He gradually earns the respect of these native people, and sheds his white-man's ways.

Dark Commander **(1940) NR**
Director: Raoul Walsh
Producer: Sol C. Siegel
Runtime: 94 Minutes
Country/Language: USA/English
Color: Black and White
Company: Republic Pictures
Distributor: Artisan Entertainment

Cowpoke Bob Seton becomes a rival for William Cantrell's girl and for the sheriff's job Cantrell covets. When Seton wins both, Cantrell forsakes his respected position as schoolteacher and leads a band of renegades through Kansas, looting and destroying, all in the name of the Confederacy.

Day Lincoln was Shot, The **(1998) NR**
Director: John Gray
Producer: Robert Greenwald
Runtime: 95 Minutes
Country/Language: USA/English
Color: Color
Company: Turner Network Television
Distributor: Turner Network Television

Summary Not Available

Drummer of the 8th, The **(1913) NR**
Director: Thomas H. Ince
Producer: Thomas H. Ince
Runtime: 24 Minutes
Country/Language: USA/English
Color: Black and White
Company: Broncho Film Company
Distributor: Image Entertainment Company

When the Civil War begins, young Billy runs away from home to enlist in the Northern Army as a drummer; he's wounded in battle and taken prisoner. He manages to escape and deliver an important message to his commanding officer, but loses his life in the process.

Drums in the Deep South **(1951) NR**
Director: William Menzies
Producer: Frank King
Runtime: 87 Minutes
Country/Language: USA/English
Color: Color

Company: King Brothers Productions
Distributor: Reel Media International

Best friends Clay Clayburn and Will Denning graduate from West Point only to soon find themselves fighting on opposite sides of the Civil War. When the two men meet each other in combat, neither knows it as each is in an artillery position hundreds of yards from the other. However, the love of Clay's life, Kathy Summers, does know and tries desperately to save her two good friends from killing each other.

E

***Escape from Fort Bravo* (1954) NR**
AKA: *Fort Bravo*
Director: John Sturges
Producer: Nicholas Nayfack
Runtime: 99 Minutes
Country/Language: USA/English
Color: Color
Company: Metro-Goldwyn-Mayer (MGM)
Distributor: MGM/UA Home Entertainment Inc.

A ruthless Union captain is renowned throughout his prison fort as the toughest soldier in the business, capable of capturing every escaped convict under his supervision. However, when he falls in love with a visiting woman some of the prisoners seize the advantage and try to escape while he is in a more 'mellow' mood.

F

***Fastest Guitar Player Alive, The* (1967) NR**
Director: Michael Moore
Producer: Sam Katzman
Runtime: 87 Minutes
Country/Language: USA/English
Color: Color

Company: Four-Leaf Productions
Distributor: Metro-Goldwyn-Mayer

The South is losing the Civil War and the coffers are nearly empty. A group of Confederate spies steal a shipment of gold in San Francisco and attempt to deliver it to a Confederate general in El Paso. Others know about the gold and seek to steal it from them, but the spies have a secret weapon: a guitar that shoots bullets.

Friendly Persuasion **(1956) NR**
Director: William Wyler
Producer: William Wyler
Runtime: 137 Minutes
Country/Language: USA/English
Color: Color
Company: Allied Artists Picture Corp.
Distributor: Allied Artists Picture Corp.

The film is about a family of Quakers in Indiana in 1862. Their religious sect is strongly opposed to violence and war. It's not easy for them to meet the rules of their religion in everyday life but when Southern troops pass the area they are in real trouble. Should they fight, despite their peaceful attitude?

Fugitive, The **(1910) NR**
Director: D.W. Griffith
Producer: D.W. Griffith
Runtime: 17 Minutes
Country/Language: USA/English
Color: Black and White
Company: Biograph Company
Distributor: Kino Video

Summary Not Available

G

Gangs of New York (2002) R
Director: Martin Scorsese
Producer: Bob Weinstein
Runtime: 166 Minutes
Country/Language: USA/English
Color: Color
Company: Miramax
Distributor: Miramax

As waves of immigrants swell the population of New York, lawlessness and corruption thrive in Manhattan's Five Points section. After years of incarceration, young Irish immigrant Amsterdam Vallon returns seeking revenge against the rival gang leader who killed his father. But Amsterdam's personal vendetta becomes part of the gang warfare that erupts as he and his fellow Irishmen fight to carve a place for themselves in their newly adopted homeland!

General, The (1927) NR
Director: Buster Keaton & Cylde Bruckman
Producer: Buster Keaton
Runtime: 75 Minutes
Country/Language: USA/English
Color: Black and White
Company: Buster Keaton Productions Inc.
Distributor: Reel Media International

Johnnie loves his train "The General" and Annabelle Lee. When the Civil War begins he is turned down for service because he's more valuable as an engineer. Annabelle thinks it's because he's a coward. Union spies capture "The General" with Annabelle on board. Johnny must rescue both his loves.

General Spanky (1936) NR
Director: G. Douglas & F. Newmeyer
Producer: Hal Roach

Runtime: 71 Minutes
Country/Language: USA/English
Color: Black and White
Company: Hal Roach Studios Inc.
Distributor: Warner Studios

A small boy is instrumental in a famous Civil War victory.

Gettysburg (1993) PG
AKA: *Killer Angels, The*
Director: Ronald Maxwell
Producer: Robert Katz
Runtime: 261 Minutes
Country/Language: USA/English
Color: Color
Company: Turner Pictures
Distributor: Warner Home Video

In 1863, the Northern and Southern forces fight at Gettysburg in the decisive battle of the American Civil War.

Glory (1989) R
Director: Edward Zwick
Producer: Freddie Fields
Runtime: 122 Minutes
Country/Language: USA/English
Color: Color
Company: Tri-Star Pictures
Distributor: Columbia Tri-Star

This film is based on the letters of Colonel Robert G. Shaw. Shaw was an officer in the Federal Army during the American Civil War who volunteered to lead the first company of black soldiers. Shaw was forced to deal with the prejudices of both the enemy (who had orders to kill commanding officers of black soldiers), and of his own fellow officers.

Gods and Generals **(2003) PG-13**
Director: Ronald Maxwell
Producer: Ted Turner
Runtime: 231 Minutes
Country/Language: USA/English
Color: Color
Company: Turner Pictures
Distributor: Warner Home Video

Gods and Generals follows the rise and fall of legendary war hero "Stonewall Jackson". The prequel to the 1993 hit *Gettysburg*.

Gone With the Wind **(1939) G**
Director: Victor Fleming
Producer: David O. Selznick
Runtime: 258 Minutes
Country/Language: USA/English
Color: Color
Company: Selznick International Pictures
Distributor: Warner Home Video

Scarlett is a woman who can deal with a nation at war, Atlanta burning, the Union Army carrying off everything from her beloved Tara, the carpetbaggers who arrive after the war. Scarlett is beautiful. She has vitality. But Ashley, the man she has wanted for so long, is going to marry his placid cousin, Melanie. Mammy warns Scarlett to behave herself at the party at Twelve Oaks. There is a new man there that day, the day the Civil War begins. Rhett Butler. Scarlett does not know he is in the room when she pleads with Ashley to choose her instead of Melanie.

Good, the Bad, and the Ugly, The **(1967) R**
AKA: *Buono, il brutto, il cattivo, Il*
Director: Sergio Leone
Producer: Alberto Grimaldi
Runtime: 180 Minutes
Country/Language: Italy/Italian
Color: Color

Company: Arturo González Producciones Cinematográficas, S.A
Distributor: MGM/UA Home Entertainment Inc.

The Good is Blondie, a wandering gunman with a strong personal sense of honor. The Bad is Angel Eyes, a sadistic hitman who always hits his mark. The Ugly is Tuco, a Mexican bandit who's only looking out for himself. Against the backdrop of the Civil War, they search for gold buried in a graveyard. Each knows only a portion of the gold's exact location, so for the moment they're dependent on each other. However, none are particularly inclined to share.

Granddad (1913) NR
Director: Thomas H. Ince
Producer: Thomas H. Ince
Runtime: 29 Minutes
Country/Language: USA/English
Color: Black and White
Company: Broncho Film Company
Distributor: Image Entertainment Company

Mildred is staying with her grandfather, Civil War veteran Jabez Burr, when she receives a letter from her father. Her father has re-married, and will be bringing his new wife home soon. But when Mildred's stepmother finds out that Jabez drinks, she takes a dislike to him, and begins to resent his closeness with Mildred. Soon Jabez decides to leave, to avoid causing further friction. He tells Mildred that he is working on a farm, but he is really staying at the county poor house. Meanwhile, a colonel whose life he saved in the war has been looking for Jabez.

Great Locomotive Chase, The (1956) NR
AKA: *Andrews' Raiders*
Director: Francis Lyon
Producer: Lawrence Watkin
Runtime: 85 Minutes
Country/Language: USA/English
Color: Color

Company: Walt Disney Productions
Distributor: Buena Vista Pictures

This film is based on a true story. During the Civil War, a Union spy, Andrews, is asked to lead a band of Union soldiers into the South so that they could destroy the railway system. However, things do not go as planned when the conductor of the train that they stole is on to them and is doing everything he can to stop them.

Guns of Fort Petticoat (1957) NR
Director: George Marshall
Producer: Harry Joe Brown
Runtime: 82 Minutes
Country/Language: USA/English
Color: Color
Company: Columbia Pictures Corporation
Distributor: Columbia Pictures

Murphy deserts the Union Army to warn former Texas neighbors of impending Indian attacks triggered by Army massacre. He overcomes initial distrust and convinces the homesteaders (all women whose men are away fighting in the Confederate Army) to take refuge in an abandoned mission. He trains them to fight and shoot in anticipation of the attack. The only other man at the mission runs away to save his scalp and ends up leading the Indians back to the mission. Surrounded and outnumbered, the defenders prepare for the final assault.

H

Hangman's Knot (1952) NR
Director: Roy Huggins
Producer: Harry Joe Brown
Runtime: 81 Minutes
Country/Language: USA/English
Color: Color
Company: Columbia Picture Corporation

Distributor: Columbia TriStar

It's 1865 in Nevada and units of rebel soldiers attack a Union troop carrying gold. They kill the soldiers and capture the gold only to learn the war ended a month ago. Deciding to keep the gold they flee but get chased by a group of drifters that want the gold. They get pinned down at a stage relay station and when deals between the two sides fail, the drifters decide to burn them out.

His Trust (1911) NR
Director: D.W. Griffith
Producer: D.W. Griffith
Runtime: 14 Minutes
Country/Language: USA/English
Color: Black and White
Company: Biograph Company
Distributor: Kino Video

A Confederate officer is called off to war. He leaves his wife and daughter in the care of George, his faithful black servant. After the officer is killed in an exciting battle sequence, George continues in his caring duties, faithful to his trust. Events continue to turn for the worse when invading Yankee soldiers arrive to loot and torch the widow's home. George saves the officer's daughter and battle sword by braving the flames.

His Trust Fulfilled (1911) NR
Director: D.W. Griffith
Producer: D.W. Griffith
Runtime: 17 Minutes
Country/Language: USA/English
Color: Black and White
Company: Biograph Company
Distributor: Kino Video

Continuing where *His Trust* (1911) leaves off, George, a slave, takes care of his deceased master's daughter after her mother's death. He sacrifices his own meager savings to give the girl a good life, until the money runs out and he tries to steal money from the girl's rich cousin.

Horses Soldier, The (1959) NR
Director: John Ford
Producer: John Mahin
Runtime: 119 Minutes
Country/Language: USA/English
Color: Color
Company: Mahin-Rackin
Distributor: MGM/UA Home Entertainment Inc.

A Union Cavalry outfit is sent behind confederate lines in strength to destroy a rail/supply centre. Along with them is sent a doctor who causes instant antipathy between him and the commander. The secret plan for the mission is overheard by a southern belle who must be taken along to assure her silence. The Union officers each have different reasons for wanting to be on the mission.

House With Closed Shutters, The (1910) NR
Director: D.W. Griffith
Producer: D.W. Griffith
Runtime: 17 Minutes
Country/Language: USA/English
Color: Black and White
Company: Biograph Company
Distributor: Image Entertainment

During the Civil War a young soldier loses his nerve in battle and runs away to his home to hide; his sister puts on his uniform, takes her brother's place in the battle, and is killed. Their mother, not wanting the shameful truth to become known, closes all the shutters (hence the film's title) and keeps her son's presence a secret for many years, though two boyhood chums stumble upon the truth.

How the West Was Won (1962) G
Director: John Ford
Producer: Bernard Smith
Runtime: 162 Minutes
Country/Language: USA/English
Color: Color
Company: Cinerama
Distributor: MGM/UA Home Entertainment Inc.

The film depicts the history of Western expansion in the United States as told by the story of one pioneer family's history. Zebulon Prescott takes his family from New York, heading west in the early 1800s. His children and grandchildren eventually reach the Western shore after years of hardship, war, and struggle.

Hunley, The (1999) NR
AKA: *C.S.S. Hunley*
Director: John Gray
Producer: Tracey Alexander
Runtime: 94 Minutes
Country/Language: USA/English
Color: Color
Company: Adelson Entertainment
Distributor: Turner Home Video

C.S.S. Hunley tells the incredible true story of the crew of the manually propelled submarine C.S.S. Hunley, during the siege of Charleston of 1864. It is a story of heroism in the face of adversity, the Hunley being the first submersible to sink an enemy boat in time of war. It also relates the human side of the story relating the uncommon and extraordinary temperament of the nine men who led the Hunley into history and died valiantly accomplishing this feat.

I

In the Border States (1910) NR
Director: D.W. Griffith

Producer: D.W. Griffith
Runtime: 17 Minutes
Country/Language: USA/English
Color: Black and White
Company: Biograph Company
Distributor: Kino Video

During the Civil War, a father living in a border state leaves to join the Union Army. After he leaves, Confederate troops forage on his property, where a soldier encounters one of his daughters. The father himself is wounded on a hazardous mission and must run for his life, pursued by Confederate soldiers.

Ironclads **(1991) PG**
Director: Delbert Mann
Producer: Ira Marvin
Runtime: N/A
Country/Language: USA/English
Color: Color
Company: N/A
Distributor: N/A

A naval battle between two large ships: the "Monitor" and the "Merrimack".

J

Jezebel **(1938) NR**
Director: William Wyler
Producer: William Wyler
Runtime: 103 Minutes
Country/Language: USA/English
Color: Black and White
Company: Warner Bros. Pictures
Distributor: Warner Home Video

Set in antebellum New Orleans during the early 1850's, this film follows Julie Marsden through her quest for social redemption on her own terms. Julie is a beautiful and free spirited, rapacious Southern belle who is sure of herself and controlling of her fiancé Preston Dillard, a successful young banker. Julie's sensitive but domineering personality (she does not want so much to hurt as to assert her independence) forces a wedge between Preston and herself. To win him back, she plays North against South amid a deadly epidemic of yellow fever which claims a surprising victim.

Journey To Shiloh **(1968) NR**
Director: William Hale
Producer: Howard Christie
Runtime: 101 minutes
Country/Language: USA/English
Color: Color
Company: Universal Pictures
Distributor: Universal Pictures

At the beginning of the Civil War, seven friends embark on a cross-country journey in order to join the Confederate army.

L

Last Samurai, The **(2003) R**
AKA: *The Last Samurai: Bushidou*
Director: Edward Zwick
Producer: Tom Cruise
Runtime: 154 Minutes
Country/Language: USA/English
Color: Color
Company: Warner Bros. Pictures
Distributor: Warner Bros. Pictures

In Japan, Civil War veteran Captain Nathan Algren trains the Emperor's troops to use modern weapons as they prepare to defeat the last of the country's samurais. But, Algren's passion is swayed when he is captured by the samurai and learns about their traditions and code of honor.

Lincoln (1988) NR
AKA: *Gore Vidal's Lincoln*
Director: Lamont Johnson
Producer: Rick Rosenberg
Runtime: 188 Minutes
Country/Language: USA/English
Color: Color
Company: Chris/Rose Productions
Distributor: N/A

Summary Not Available

Little Colonel, The (1935) NR
Director: David Butler
Producer: Buddy G. DeSylva
Runtime: 80 Minutes
Country/Language: USA/English
Color: Black and White
Company: Fox Film Corporation
Distributor: Fox Video

After southern belle Elizabeth Lloyd runs off to marry Yankee Jack Sherman, her father, a former Confederate colonel during the Civil War, vows to never speak to her again. Several years pass and Elizabeth returns to her hometown with her husband and young daughter. The little girl charms her crusty grandfather and tries to patch things up between him and her mother.

Little Women (1933) NR
Director: George Cukor
Producer: Merian Cooper
Runtime: 117 Minutes
Country/Language: USA/English
Color: Black and White
Company: RKO Radio Pictures
Distributor: Warner Home Video

With their father away fighting in the Civil War, Joe, Meg, Beth and Amy grow up with their mother in somewhat reduced circumstances. They are a close family, who inevitably has their squabbles and tragedies. But the bond holds even when, later, men friends start to become a part of the household.

Littlest Rebel, The (1935) PG
Director: David Butler
Producer: Buddy G. DeSylva
Runtime: 70 Minutes
Country/Language: USA/English
Color: Black and White
Company: Twentieth Century-Fox Film Corporation
Distributor: Fox Video

Shirley Temple's father, a rebel officer, sneaks back to his rundown plantation to see his family and is arrested. A Yankee takes pity and sets up an escape. Everyone is captured and the officers are to be executed. Shirley and "Bojangles" Robinson beg President Lincoln to intercede.

Love Me Tender (1957) NR
AKA: *Reno Brothers, The*
Director: Robert Webb
Producer: David Weisbart
Runtime: 89 Minutes
Country/Language: USA/English
Color: Black and White
Company: 20th Century Fox
Distributor: Fox Video

Elvis plays Clint Reno, one of the Reno brothers who stayed home while his brother went to fight in the Civil War for the Confederate army. When his brother Vance comes back from the war, he finds that his old girlfriend Cathy has married Clint. The family has to struggle to reach stability with this issue. Vance is involved in a train robbery, while a Confederate soldier, of Federal Government money. There is a conflict of interest, when Vance tries to return the money, against the wishes of some of his fellow Confederates.

M

Macho Callahan (1970) R
Director: Bernard Kowalski
Producer: Martin Schute
Runtime: 99 Minutes
Country/Language: Mexico & USA/English
Color: Color
Company: Felicidad Productions
Distributor: MGM/UA Home Entertainment Inc.

A man tricked into enlisting in the Confederate army is later thrown into a hellish stockade on desertion charges. He eventually breaks out of the prison camp, reunites with his old partner and sets out to kill the man who was responsible for his being in the camp in the first place. However, after accidentally killing a Confederate officer, he finds himself pursued by a gang of vicious bounty hunters intent on collecting the reward put up by the dead officer's widow.

Major Dundee (1965) PG-13
Director: Sam Peckinpah
Producer: Jerry Bresler
Runtime: 117 Minutes
Country/Language: USA/English
Color: Color
Company: Columbia Pictures Corporation
Distributor: Columbia Pictures Home Video

During the last winter of the Civil War, cavalry officer Amos Dundee leads a contentious troop of Army regulars, Confederate prisoners and scouts on an expedition into Mexico to destroy a band of Apaches who have been raiding U.S. bases in Texas.

Man from Colorado, The **(1967) NR**
Director: Henry Levin
Producer: Jules Schermer
Runtime: 100 Minutes
Country/Language: USA/English
Color: Color
Company: Columbia Pictures Corporation
Distributor: Columbia Pictures Home Video

Two friends return home after their discharge from the army after the Civil War. However, one of them has had deep-rooted psychological damage due to his experiences during the war, and as his behavior becomes more erratic and violent, his friend desperately tries to find a way to help him.

Mosby's Marauders **(1967) NR**
AKA: *Willie and the Yank*
Director: Michael O'Herlihy
Producer: Bill Anderson
Runtime: 79 Minutes
Country/Language: USA/English
Color: Color
Company: Walt Disney Pictures
Distributor: N/A

Summary Not Available

N

North and South **(1985) NR**
Director: Richard Heffron
Producer: David Wolper
Runtime: 561 Minutes
Country/Language: USA/English
Color: Color
Company: Warner Bros. Television
Distributor: American Broadcasting Company

Based on John Jakes best selling novel this is the story of the friendship between two boys, George Hazard and Orry Main, that meet at West Point. George is from a wealthy Pennsylvania steel family and Orry is from a Southern plantation where his family keeps slaves. In the years leading up to the Civil War their friendship is tested as their families interact and hostilities between the North and South increase.

***North and South, Book II* (1986) NR**
Director: Kevin Conner
Producer: David Wolper
Runtime: 570 Minutes
Country/Language: USA/English
Color: Color
Company: Warner Bros. Television
Distributor: American Broadcasting Company

This film is the continuing saga of the Hazards and the Mains. The Hazards are from the North and the Mains from the South. George Hazard and Orry Main met at West Point and fought in the Mexican American war together becoming fast friends. Now they find themselves fighting on opposite sides of the Civil War and struggle to maintain their friendship through these troubled times.

***North and South, Book III* (1994) NR**
AKA: *Heaven & Hell: North & South, Book III*
Director: Larry Peerce
Producer: Hal Galli
Runtime: 261 Minutes
Country/Language: USA/English
Color: Color
Company: Warner Bros. Television
Distributor: American Broadcasting Company

This film is the final installment in John Jakes trilogy of the Civil War. It focuses on the Reconstruction period and the continuing saga of the Hazards (from the North) and the Mains (from the South). Both families face the deaths of loved ones at the hands of old enemies. The action moves to the old west as Charles Main becomes a cavalry officer.

O

***Occurrence at Owl Creek Bridge, An* (1930) NR**
AKA: *Rivière du hibou, La*
Director: Robert Enrico
Producer: Marcel Ichac
Runtime: 25 Minutes
Country/Language: France/French
Color: Black and White
Company: Filmartic
Distributor: Festival Films

A Civil War soldier is to be executed by hanging, but when the plank is kicked away, instead of breaking his neck, he manages to miraculously escape unscathed or did he?

***Of Human Hearts* (1938) NR**
Director: Clarence Brown
Producer: Clarence Brown
Runtime: 103 Minutes
Country/Language: USA/English
Color: Black and White
Company: Metro-Goldwyn-Mayer (MGM)
Distributor: MGM/UA Home Entertainment Inc.

This is a story about family relationships, set in the time before and during the American Civil War. Ethan Wilkins is a poor and honest man who ministers to the human soul, while his son Jason yearns to be a doctor, helping people in the earthly realm. It is a rich story about striving for excellence, the tension of father-son rebellion, and the love of a mother that can never die.

***Oldest Living Confederate Widow Tells All, The* (1990) NR**
Director: Ken Cameron
Producer: Larry Sanitsky

Runtime: 170 Minutes
Country/Language: Australia/English
Color: Color
Company: Konigsberg/Sanitsky Company
Distributor: CBS Television

Summary Not Available

***Outlaw Josey Wales, The* (1976) PG**
Director: Clinton Eastwood
Producer: Robert Daley
Runtime: 135 Minutes
Country/Language: USA/English
Color: Color
Company: The Malpaso Company
Distributor: Warner Home Video

Josey Wales makes his way west after the Civil War, determined to live a useful and helpful life. He joins up with a group of settlers who need the protection that a man as tough and experienced as he is can provide. Unfortunately, the past has a way of catching up with you, and Josey is a wanted man.

P

***Pharaoh's Army* (1995) PG-13**
Director: Robert Henson
Producer: Robert Henson
Runtime: 90 Minutes
Country/Language: USA/English
Color: Color
Company: Cicada Films
Distributor: Orion Home Entertainment Corp.

During the American Civil War, a Union Army captain leads his rag-tag cavalry troop up a misty creek to a remote farm to steal enemy (Confederate) livestock. The farm is worked by Sarah Anders, whose husband is away fighting for the Confederate Army.

Far from the great armies and battlefields, a very private civil war erupts. The Captain and Sarah are pulled apart by the war's undertow into choices they can not fully control or understand. Each character in this drama must decide whether loyalty will be paid in blood. This story has a relevance to current partisan conflicts. Armies are not filled with murdering psychopaths. Good people can be driven to do bad things. The story chronicles the pathology of war, how escalating events can trigger unasked-for tragedy. This film is based on a true story about a southern child who shot and killed a union soldier during the Civil War.

Private History of a Campaign That Failed, The (1981) NR
Director: Peter H. Hunt
Producer: Peter H. Hunt
Runtime: 89 Minutes
Country/Language: USA/English
Color: Color
Company: Nebraska Educational Television
Distributor: Public Broadcasting Service

Mark Twain's tale of cowardly Confederate soldiers.

Proud Rebel, The (1958) NR
Director: Michael Curtiz
Producer: Samuel Goldwyn Jr.
Runtime: 103 Minutes
Country/Language: USA/English
Color: Color
Company: Formosa
Distributor: HBO Home Video

Searching for a doctor who can help him get his son to speak again (because the boy had not uttered a word since he saw his mother die in the fire that burned down the family home), a Confederate veteran finds himself facing a 30-day jail sentence when he is unfairly accused of starting a brawl in a small town. A local woman pays his fine, providing that he works it off on her ranch. He soon finds himself involved in the woman's struggle to keep her ranch from a local landowner who wants it and whose sons were responsible for the man being framed for the fight.

R

Raintree County (1957) NR
Director: Edward Dmytryk
Producer: David Lewis
Runtime: 182 Minutes
Country/Language: USA/English
Color: Color
Company: Metro-Goldwyn-Mayer (MGM)
Distributor: Warner Bros. Television

Idealist John Wickliff Shawnessy drifts away from his high school sweetheart Nell Gaither and enters into a passionate, but loveless, marriage with Susanna Drake a wealthy New Orleans belle. But John soon learns that Susanna's mother died in a lunatic asylum and it becomes apparent that Susanna has inherited her family's curse for she tricked him into marriage. Frustrated with life, John leaves home by enlisting in the Northern Army and fights in Tennessee and Georgia during the terrible and brutal Civil War where he does some soul searching for himself and explores his path in life to what may lay in store for him should he return home.

Red Badge of Courage, The (1951) NR
Director: John Houston
Producer: Gottfried Reinhardt
Runtime: 69 Minutes
Country/Language: USA/English
Color: Black and White
Company: Metro-Goldwyn-Mayer (MGM)
Distributor: MGM/UA Home Entertainment Inc.

The plot centers around a young recruit who faces the horrors of war. He vacillates between wanting to fight and doubting his own courage. In midst of first bloody encounter, he runs away. After seeing the dead and wounded, a sense of shame leads him back to his unit, where he distinguishes himself in the next battle. Having overcome his fear of death he knows he can face whatever comes.

***Ride With the Devil* (1999) R**
AKA: *Civil War*
Director: Ang Lee
Producer: David Linde
Runtime: 138 Minutes
Country/Language: USA/English
Color: Color
Company: Universal Pictures
Distributor: Universal Pictures

Jake Roedel and Jack Bull Chiles are friends in Missouri when the Civil War starts. Women and blacks know their place. Jack Bull's dad is killed by Union soldiers, so the young men join the Bushwhackers, irregulars loyal to the South. One is a black man, Daniel Holt, beholden to the man who bought his freedom. They skirmish then spend long hours hiding. Sue Lee, a young widow, brings them food. She and Jack Bull become lovers, and when he's grievously wounded, Jake escorts her south to a safe farm. The Bushwhackers, led by men set on revenge, make a raid into Kansas. At 19, Jake is ill at ease with war. As his friends die one after another, he must decide where honor lies.

***Rio Lobo* (1970) R**
AKA: *San Timoteo*
Director: Howard Hawks
Producer: Howard Hawks
Runtime: 114 Minutes
Country/Language: USA/English
Color: Color
Company: Malabar
Distributor: Paramount Home Video

Col. Cord McNally an ex-union officer teams up with a couple of ex Johnny Rebs to search for the traitor who sold information to the South during the Civil War. Their quest brings them to the town of Rio Lobo where they help recover this little Texas town from ruthless outlaws who are led by the traitor they were looking for.

Roots **(1977) NR**
Director: Marvin Chomsky & John Erman
Producer: David Wolper
Runtime: 573 Minutes
Country/Language: USA/English
Color: Color
Company: Warner Bros. Television
Distributor: Warner Bros. Television

This film is a saga of African-American life, based on Alex Haley's family history. Kunta Kinte is abducted from his African village, sold into slavery, and taken to America. He makes several escape attempts until he is finally caught and maimed. He marries Bell, his plantation's cook, and they have a daughter, Kizzy, who is eventually sold away from them. Kizzy has a son by her new master, and the boy grows up to become Chicken George, a legendary cock fighter who leads his family into freedom. Throughout the series, the family observes notable events in U.S. history, such as the Revolutionary and Civil Wars, slave uprisings, and emancipation.

Rose and the Jackal, The **(1990) PG**
Director: Jack Gold
Producer: Steve White
Runtime: 100 Minutes
Country/Language: USA/English
Color: Color
Company: Turner Network Television
Distributor: N/A

Union detective Allan Pinkerton falls in love with an aristocrat caught spying for the Confederacy.

S

***Santa Fe Trail* (1940) NR**
Director: Michael Curtiz
Producer: Hal Wallis
Runtime: 110 Minutes
Country/Language: USA/English
Color: Black and White
Company: Warner bros. Pictures
Distributor: Reel Media International

The story of Jeb Stewart, his romance with Kit Carson Holliday, friendship with George Custer and battles against John Brown in the days leading up to the outbreak of the American Civil War.

***Seven Angry Men* (1955) NR**
AKA: *God's Angry Men*
Director: Charles Marquis Warren
Producer: Vincent M. Fennelly
Runtime: 90 Minutes
Country/Language: USA/English
Color: Black and White
Company: Allied Artists Pictures Corporation
Distributor: Allied Artists Pictures Corporation

The rise, fall, and execution of John Brown.

***Shenandoah* (1965) NR**
Director: Andrew McLaglen
Producer: Robert Arthur
Runtime: 105 Minutes
Country/Language: USA/English
Color: Color
Company: Universal Pictures

Distributor: Universal Home Entertainment

Charlie Anderson is a farmer in Shenandoah, Virginia and finds himself (and his family) in the middle of the Civil War. He decides not to get involved in the war because he believes that this is not "his" war. But he eventually has to get involved when his youngest boy is taken prisoner by the North.

So the Red Rose (1935) NR
Director: King Vidor
Producer: Douglas MacLean
Runtime: Minutes
Country/Language: USA/English
Color: Black and White
Company: Paramount Pictures
Distributor: Paramount Pictures

So Red the Rose is King Vidor's quietly affecting Civil War romance, starring Margaret Sullavan as a Southern aristocrat, the mistress of a Southern plantation, whose sheltered life is torn apart by the War Between the States. During the war's darkest days she is sustained by her love for a distant cousin, a Confederate officer, played by Randolph Scott.

South of St. Louis (1964) NR
AKA: *Distant Drums*
Director: Ray Enright
Producer: Milton Sperling
Runtime: 88 Minutes
Country/Language: USA/English
Color: Color
Company: United States Pictures
Distributor: Warner Bros. Pictures

Summary Not Available

Southern Yankee, A (1948)
AKA: *My Hero*

Director: Edward Sedgwick
Producer: Paul Jones
Runtime: 90 Minutes
Country/Language: USA/English
Color: Black and White
Company: Metro-Goldwyn-Mayer (MGM)
Distributor: MGM/UA Home Entertainment Inc.

Aubrey Filmore is a bumbling bellboy in a Missouri town who pesters the Union officers there; he desperately wants to be a spy for the North in the American Civil War. When Filmore accidentally waylays an infamous Confederate spy known as "The Grey Spider" and is mistaken for him by the Rebels, the Union brass see it as an opportunity for real espionage, and though Filmore is a coward as well as a fool, his real motivation is a sweet Southern girl named Sallyann, whom he will see again behind Southern lines.

Springfield Rifle (1952) NR
Director: Andre' De Toth
Producer: Louis Edelman
Runtime: 93 Minutes
Country/Language: USA/English
Color: Color
Company: Warner Bros. Pictures
Distributor: Warner Bros. Pictures

Major Lex Kearney, dishonorably discharged from the army for cowardice in battle, has actually volunteered to go undercover to try to prevent raids against shipments of horses desperately needed for the Union war effort. Falling in with the gang of jayhawkers and Confederate soldiers who have been conducting the raids, he gradually gains their trust and is put in a position where he can discover who has been giving them secret information revealing the routes of the horse shipments.

Swords and Hearts (1911) NR
Director: D.W. Griffith

Producer: D.W. Griffith
Runtime: 17 Minutes
Country/Language: USA/English
Color: Black and White
Company: Biograph Company
Distributor: Kino Video

A poor girl is secretly in love with a wealthy young planter. During the Civil War she helps him escape capture by Union soldiers. After the war, with his fortune gone, she confesses that she loves him.

T

***Tennessee Johnson* (1942)**
AKA: *The Man on America's Conscience*
Director: William Dieterle
Producer: J. Walter Ruben
Runtime: 103 Minutes
Country/Language: USA/English
Color: Black and White
Company: Metro-Goldwyn-Mayer (MGM)
Distributor: Metro-Goldwyn-Mayer (MGM)

Summary Not Available

***Their One Love* (1915) NR**
Director: Jack Harvey
Producer: Jack Harvey
Runtime: 15 Minutes
Country/Language: USA/English
Color: Black and White
Company: Thanhouser Film Corporation
Distributor: Mutual Film Corporation

In the 1850s twin girls fall in love with the same young man, and must struggle with their feelings once he goes off to fight in the Civil War.

They Died With Their Boots On **(1941) NR**
AKA: *To The Last Man*
Director: Raoul Walsh
Producer: Hal Wallis
Runtime: 140 Minutes
Country/Language: USA/English
Color: Black and White
Company: Warner Bros. Pictures
Distributor: MGM/UA Home Entertainment Inc.

This is the story of General Custer from the time he enters West Point military academy, through the American Civil War, and finally to his death at Little Big Horn. The battle against Chief Crazy Horse is portrayed as a crooked deal between politicians and a corporation which wants the land Custer gave to the Indians.

U

Undefeated, The **(1969) G**
Director: Andrew McLaglen
Producer: Robert Jacks
Runtime: 119 Minutes
Country/Language: USA/English
Color: Color
Company: 20th Century Fox
Distributor: Fox Video

After the Civil War, ex-Union Colonel John Henry Thomas and ex-Confederate Colonel James Langdon are leading two desperate groups of people through strife-torn Mexico. John Henry and company are bringing horses to the unpopular Mexican government for $35 a head while Langdon is leading a contingent of displaced southerners, who are looking for a new life in Mexico after losing their property to carpetbaggers. The two men are eventually forced to mend their differences in order to fight off both bandits and revolutionaries, as they try to lead their friends and kin to safety.

V

Virginia City (1940) NR
Director: Michael Curtiz
Producer: Hal Wallis
Runtime: 118 Minutes
Country/Language: USA/English
Color: Black and White
Company: Warner Bros. Pictures
Distributor: Warner Home Video

Union officer Kerry Bradford escapes from Confederate Prison and is headed to Virginia City in Nevada. Once there he finds that the former commander of his prison Vance Irby is planning to send $5 million in gold to save the Confederacy.

W

Wicked Spring (2002) PG-13
Director: Kevin Hershberger
Producer: Kevin Hershberger
Runtime: 102 Minutes
Country/Language: USA/English
Color: Color
Company: Wicked Springs LLC
Distributor: Ardustry Home Entertainment

During the 1864 battle of the Wilderness, three Union soldiers and three Confederate Soldiers get separated from their units as twilight engulfs the ravaged battlefield. The men wander alone through the dangerous woods, separate of each other, until they meet by chance on the banks of a quiet creek. The men meet and spend the night around a campfire, not realizing they are enemies until the next morning when the sun rises and a new day of battle begins.

Y

Young Mr. Lincoln **(1939) NR**
Director: John Ford
Producer: Darryl Zanuck
Runtime: 100 Minutes
Country/Language: USA/English
Color: Black and White
Company: Twentieth Century Fox
Distributor: Criterion Collection

Ten years in the life of Abraham Lincoln, before he became known to his nation and the world. He moves from a Kentucky cabin to Springfield, Illinois, to begin his law practice. He defends two men accused of murder in a political brawl, suffers the death of his girlfriend Ann, courts his future wife Mary Todd, and agrees to go into politics.

Notes

*Information courtesy of The Internet Movie Database (http://www.imdb.com). Used with permission.

**Individuals are responsible for determining the appropriateness of each film for use in the classroom.

FOUR

INTERVIEW WITH JAMES McPHERSON

About James McPherson

James M. McPherson was born in North Dakota and raised in Minnesota. He graduated from Gustavus Adolphus College in 1958 and earned his Ph.D. from Johns Hopkins University in 1963. He taught at Princeton University from 1962 - 2004, and is now the George Henry Davis '86 Professor of American History Emeritus at Princeton University.

Dr. McPherson has authored more than 15 books and has edited several more. He has won numerous awards for his scholarship, most notably the Pulitzer Prize in 1989 for, *Battle Cry of Freedom: The Civil War Era* and the Lincoln Prize for, *For Cause and Comrades: Why Men Fought in the Civil War*.

In 2000, he gave the National Endowment for the Humanities Jefferson Lecture at the Kennedy Center. He has also served as the president of the Society for American History (1999-2000) and the American Historical Association (2003-04).

James McPherson is a well-known civil war historian and is considered by many to be the world's foremost scholar on the Civil War.

William Russell (WR): Dr. McPherson, what is your favorite Civil War movie? Why?

James McPherson (JM): *Red Badge of Courage*, because of its sensitive exploration of the psychology of a young and frightened soldier going into his first battle. One might object, however, that it is not really a Civil War movie--the war is scarcely mentioned, and the movie could almost have been about any war. Of explicitly Civil War movies, my favorite is *Glory* because it is the first (and still the only, I believe) film to present the story of black soldiers.

WR: If you could make a movie about any aspect of the Civil War, what would you focus on?

JM: Lincoln's travails as commander in chief. Steven Spielberg is reportedly making a movie about Lincoln, but I'll believe it when I see it.

WR: In your opinion, what Civil War movie is the most historically accurate? Why?

JM: Probably *Glory*. There are errors in it, but its distortions of reality are probably less than those of any other Civil War movie.

WR: What other Civil War movies do you consider historically accurate?

JM: *Gettysburg* is also pretty accurate, though of course it is based on a novel whose author exercised a certain amount of literary license.

WR: Can movies teach history?

JM: Yes, if they are done well they can both <u>teach</u> some history and also arouse an interest in the viewer that sends him/her to additional sources on the subject of the movie.

WR: Are Civil War movies more superior to a book as a communicator of feeling and understanding? If so, how?

JM: Probably superior as a communicator of feeling, but not necessarily of understanding. Movies can arouse emotions more than a book, usually, but they are less effective in communicating complexity, nuance, etc. than a book.

WR: Do Civil War movies fail to match the potential of written history? If so, how?

JM: As said in the last question, movies can arouse emotions more than a book, usually, but they are less effective in communicating complexity, nuance, etc. than a book.

WR: How much education should we expect from Civil War movies?

JM: We should expect some education, but even with good movies the education usually comes in second to entertainment.

WR: What advice would you give educators in regard to teaching the Civil War with movies?

JM: Have a Q & A session after the students see the movie, and use the answers to point out inaccuracies, distortions, etc. and to urge students to do some reading on the same subject.

WR: What advice would you give to movie makers in regard to making movies about the Civil War?

JM: Hire good historians as consultants and pay some attention to what they say.

Note
*This interview was conducted in the April of 2007 via the Internet and was printed with written permission from James M. McPherson.

APPENDIX A

Film Ratings

A G-rated motion picture contains nothing in theme, language, nudity, sex, violence or other matters that, in the view of the Rating Board, would offend parents whose younger children view the motion picture. The G rating is not a "certificate of approval," nor does it signify a "children's" motion picture. Some snippets of language may go beyond polite conversation but they are common everyday expressions. No stronger words are present in G-rated motion pictures. Depictions of violence are minimal. No nudity, sex scenes or drug use are present in the motion picture.

A PG-rated motion picture should be investigated by parents before they let their younger children attend. The PG rating indicates, in the view of the Rating Board, that parents may consider some material unsuitable for their children, and parents should make that decision.

The more mature themes in some PG-rated motion pictures may call for parental guidance. There may be some profanity and some depictions of violence or brief nudity. But these elements are not deemed so intense as to require that parents be strongly cautioned beyond the suggestion of parental guidance. There is no drug use content in a PG-rated motion picture.

PG-13 | PARENTS STRONGLY CAUTIONED
Some Material May Be Inappropriate for Children Under 13

A PG-13 rating is a sterner warning by the Rating Board to parents to determine whether their children under age 13 should view the motion picture, as some material might not be suited for them. A PG-13 motion picture may go beyond the PG rating in theme, violence, nudity, sensuality, language, adult activities or other elements, but does not reach the restricted R category. The theme of the motion picture by itself will not result in a rating greater than PG-13, although depictions of activities related to a mature theme may result in a restricted rating for the motion picture. Any drug use will initially require at least a PG-13 rating. More than brief nudity will require at least a PG-13 rating, but such nudity in a PG-13 rated motion picture generally will not be sexually oriented. There may be depictions of violence in a PG-13 movie, but generally not both realistic and extreme or persistent violence. A motion picture's single use of one of the harsher sexually-derived words, though only as an expletive, initially requires at least a PG-13 rating. More than one such expletive requires an R rating, as must even one of those words used in a sexual context. The Rating Board nevertheless may rate such a motion picture PG-13 if, based on a special vote by a two-thirds majority, the Raters feel that most American parents would believe that a PG-13 rating is appropriate because of the context or manner in which the words are used or because the use of those words in the motion picture is inconspicuous.

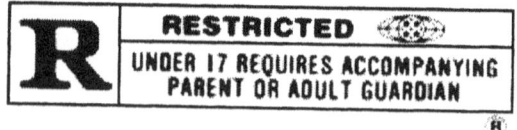

An R-rated motion picture, in the view of the Rating Board, contains some adult material. An R-rated motion picture may include adult themes, adult activity, hard language, intense or persistent violence, sexually-oriented nudity, drug abuse or other elements, so that parents are counseled to take this rating very seriously. Children under 17 are not allowed to attend R-rated motion

Appendix A

pictures unaccompanied by a parent or adult guardian. Parents are strongly urged to find out more about R-rated motion pictures in determining their suitability for their children. Generally, it is not appropriate for parents to bring their young children with them to R-rated motion pictures.

An NC-17 rated motion picture is one that, in the view of the Rating Board, most parents would consider patently too adult for their children 17 and under. No children will be admitted. NC-17 does not mean "obscene" or "pornographic" in the common or legal meaning of those words, and should not be construed as a negative judgment in any sense. The rating simply signals that the content is appropriate only for an adult audience. An NC-17 rating can be based on violence, sex, aberrational behavior, drug abuse or any other element that most parents would consider too strong and therefore off-limits for viewing by their children.

Note
*Information courtesy of the Motion Picture Association of America (www.mpaa.org). Used with permission.

REFERENCES

Allen, M. (2005). 'It is as it was': Feature films in the history classroom. *The Social Studies, 96 (2),* 61-67.

Allen, W. (1955). Research on film use: student preparation. *AV Communication Review, 5,* 423-450.

Burns, K. (Producer & Director). (1990). *The Civil War.* [Documentary]. United States. PBS Home Video

Chadwick, B. (2001). *The reel Civil War: Mythmaking in American film.* New York, NY: Knopf.

Driscoll, M.P. (2005). *Psychology of learning for instruction.* Needham Heights, MA: Allyn & Bacon.

Engle, S.H. (2003). Decision-making: The heart of social studies instruction. *The Social Studies, (94) 1*: 7-10 (Reprinted with permission from *Social Education, 27 (4),* November. P. 301-304.)

Internet Movie Database. (2007). *Internet Movie Database.* Retrieved January 18, 2007, from http://www.imdb.com

Matz, K.A. & Pingatore, L.L. (2005). Reel to reel: Teaching the twentieth century with classic Hollywood films. *Social Education, 69(4),* 189-192.

Motion Picture Association of America. (2007). *Film Ratings.* Retrieved July 25, 2007, from http://mpaa.org/FlmRat_Ratings.asp

National Center for History in Schools. (1994). *National standards for history thinking.* Retrieved January 11th, 2007, from http://nchs.ucla.edu/standards/thinking5-12.html

O'Conner, J.E. & Jackson, M.A. (1988). *American history/American film.* New York, NY: Ungar Publishing Company.

Paris, M. (1997). *ERIC clearinghouse for social studies/social science Education.* Bloomington, Indiana. (ERIC Document Reproduction Service No. EDOSO9714).

Reform K-12. (2006). *Aren't classroom VCRs wonderful? Reform K-12.* Retrieved September 7th, 2006, from http://www.reformk12.com/archives/000034.nclk

Rosenstone, R.A. (1995). *Visions of the past: The challenge of film to our idea of history.* Cambridge, MA: Harvard University Press.

Russell, W. (2007). *Using film in the Social Studies.* Lanham, MD: University Press of America.

Spehr, P.C. (1961). *The Civil War in motion pictures: A bibliography of films produced in the United States since 1897.* Washington D.C.: U.S. Government Printing Office.

United States Copyright Office. (1976). *Title 17 (1) Section 107 of the Copyright Law of the United States; Limitations on exclusive rights: Fair use.* Retrieved January 18, 2007, from http://www.copyright.gov/title17/92chap1.html#107

———. (1976). *Title 17 (1) Section 110 of the Copyright Law of the United States; Limitations on exclusive rights: Exemption of certain performances and displays.* Retrieved January 18, 2007, from http://www.copyright.gov/title17/92chap1.html#110

United States Government. (1981). Federal guidelines for off-air recording of broadcast programming for educational purposes. *Congressional Record*, pp. E4750-E4752.

INDEX

Abe Lincoln in Illinois, 16
Abraham Lincoln, 16-17
Alexander, T., 35
Allen, M., 2, 3, 5
Allen, W., 6
Alvarez Kelly, 17
Anderson, Bill, 41
Andersonville, 17
Andersonville Trial, The, 17-18
Appendix A, 61-63
Arizona Bushwhackers, The, 18
Arizona Kid, The, 18
Arthur, R., 49
Autobiography of Miss Jane Pittman, The, 19
Band of Angels, 19
Barry, Philip, 19
Battle, The, 19-20
Beguiled, The, 20
Bresler, J., 40
Beulah Land, 20
Birth of a Nation, The, 21
Blood and Honor, 21
Blue and the Gray, The, 21-22
Brown, C., 43
Brown, H.J., 32
Bruckman, Clyde, 28
Burns, K., 15
Butler, David, 38, 39
Calvary Charge, 22
Cameron, K., 43
Chadwick, B., 1, 2, 15
Charlotte Forten's Mission, 22-23

Christie, H., 37
Civil War, The, 15
Civil War Diary, 23
Civil War on Film, 1-2
Chomsky, M., 48
Class of '61, 23
Cold Mountain, 23-24
Connor, K., 42
Cooper, M., 38
Copyright, 11-13
Costner, Kevin, 24
Crane, Barry, 22
Creation of Film, 1
Cromwell, John, 16
Cruise, Tom, 37
Cukor, G., 38
Curtiz, M., 45, 49, 54
Daley, R., 44
Dances with Wolves, 24
Dark Commander, 24-25
Day Lincoln was Shot, The, 25
Days of '61, 2
David, Ray, 17
DeSylva, B., 38, 39
DeToth, A., 51
Dieterle, W., 52
Dmytryk, Edward, 17, 46
Douglas, G., 28
Driscoll, M.P., 2
Drummer of the 8th, The, 25
Drums in the Deep South, 25-26
Eastman, George, 1
Eastwood, Clinton, 44

Edelman, L., 51
Edison, Thomas, 1
Engle, Shirley, 2
Enrico, Robert, 43
Enright, R., 50
Erman, J., 48
Escape from Fort Bravo, 26
Fagan, Maurice, 21
Fair Use, 12-14
Falk, Harry, 20
Farmer, Donald, 21
Fastest Guitar Player Alive, The, 26-27
Fennelly, V., 49
Fields, F., 29
Film Ratings, 61-63
Film Use
    How to use, 5-10
Filmography, 15-52
    A, 16-19
    B, 19-22
    C, 22-24
    D, 24-26
    E, 26
    F, 26-27
    G, 28-32
    H, 32-35
    I, 35-36
    J, 36-37
    L, 37-40
    M, 40-41
    N, 41-43
    O, 43-44
    P, 44-46
    R, 46-49
    S, 49-52
    T, 52-53
    U, 53
    V, 54
    W, 54
    Y, 55

Fleming, Victor, 30
Ford, John, 34, 35, 55
Foster, Lewis, 22
Frankenheimer, J., 17
Freedman, Lewis, 17
Friendly Persuasion, 27
Fugitive, The, 27
Galli, H., 42
Gangs of New York, 28
General, The, 28
General Spanky, 28-29
Gerber, David, 20
Gettysburg, 29
Glory, 29
Gods And Generals, 30
Gold, J., 48
Goldwyn, S., 45
Gone with the Wind, 30
Good, the Bad, and the Ugly, The, 30-31
Gordon, Max, 16
Granddad, 31
Gray, J., 25, 35
Great Locomotive Chase, The, 31-32
Greenwald, R., 25
Griffith, D.W., 16, 19, 21, 27, 33, 34, 35, 36, 51, 52
Grimaldi, A., 30
Guns of Fort Petticoat, 32
Hale, W., 37
Hangman's Knot, 32-33
Harvey, Jack, 52
Hawks, H., 47
Heffron, R., 41
Henson, R., 44
Herschberger, K., 54
His Trust, 33
His Trust Fulfilled, 33-34
Hoblit, G., 23
Horses Soldier, The, 34

Houses with Closed Shutters, The, 34
Houston, J., 46
How the West was Won, 35
How to use film, 5-10
    Russell Model, 6-10
Huggins, R., 32
Hunley, The, 35
Hunt, P.H., 45
Ichac, Marcel, 43
Internet Movie Database, 55
In the Border States, 35-36
Ince, Thomas, 25, 31
Interview w/James McPherson, 57-59
    About James McPherson, 57
    Interview, 57-59
Introduction, 1-4
    Civil War on Film, 1-2
    Using Civil War Films, 2-4
Ironclads, 36
Jacks, R., 53
Jackson, M.A., 2
Jezebel, 36-37
Johnson, L., 38
Jones, P., 51
Journey to Shiloh, 37
Kane, Joseph, 18
Katz, R., 29
Katzman, S., 26
Keaton, Buster, 28
Kinetoscope, 1
King, Frank, 25
Korty, John, 19
Kowalski, B., 40
Last Samurai, The, 37
Lee, Ang, 47
Legal Issues, 11-14
    Copyright, 11-13
    Fair Use, 12-14
    Off-Air Recording of Broadcast, 13-14
Leone, Sergio, 30
Levin, H., 41
Lewis, D., 46
Lincoln, 38
Linde, D., 47
Little Colonel, The, 38
Little Women, 38-39
Littlest Rebel, The, 39
Love Me Tender, 39-40
Lyles, A.C., 18
Lyon, F., 31
Macho Callahan, 40
Mahin, J., 34
Major Dundee, 40
MacLean, D., 50
Man from Colorado, The, 41
Mann, D., 36
Marshall, G., 32
Marvin, I., 36
Matz, K.A., 2
Maxwell, R., 30
McLaglen, Andrew, 21, 49, 53
McPherson, James, 57-59
Menzies, W., 25
Meyer, Kevin, 23
Minghella, A., 23
Moore, M., 26
Motion Picture Association of America (MPAA), 61-63
Mosby's Marauders, 41
Movie Friday, 5
National Center for History in Schools, 3
National History Standards, 3
Nayfack, N., 26
Newmeyer, F., 28
North and South, 41-42
North and South, Book II, 42
North and South, Book III, 42-43
O'Conner, J.E., 2

O'Herlihy, M., 41
Occurrence at Owl Creek Bridge, An, 43
Of Human Hearts, 43
Off-Air Recording of Broadcast, 13-14
Oldest Living Confederate Tells All, 43-44
Outlaw Josey Wales, The, 44
Paris, Michael, 2
Peckinpah, S., 40
Peerce, L., 42
Peters, R.C., 23
Pharaoh's Army, 44-45
Pine, William, 22
Pingatore, L.L., 2
Private History of a Campaign that Failed, 45
Proud Rebel, The, 45-46
Raintree County, 46
Red Badge of Courage, 46-47
References, 55-56
Reform K-12, 5
Reinhardt, G., 46
Ride with the Devil, 47
Rio Lobo, 47-48
Roach, Hal, 28
Roots, 48
Rose and the Jackal, The, 48-49
Rosenberg, R., 38
Rosenstone, R.A., 2
Ruben, J.W., 52
Russell Model, 6-10
Sanitsky, L., 43
Santa Fe Trail, 49
Schermer, J., 41
School/District Film Policies, 11
Schute, Martin, 40
Scott, George, 17
Scorsese, Martin, 28
Sedgwick, E., 51

Selander, Lesley, 18
Selznick, David, 30
Seven Angry Men, 49
Shenandoah, 49-50
Siegel, Don, 20
Siegel, S.C., 24
Silent Film Era, 1-2
Smith, Bernard, 35
Spielberg, Steven, 23
So the Red Rose, 50
South of St. Louis, 50
Southern Yankee, A, 50-51
Spehr, P.C., 2
Sperling, M., 50
Springfield Rifle, 51
Sturges, J., 26
Swords and Hearts, 51-52
Teaching with Film, 5-14
    Russell Model, 5-10
    Legal Issues, 11-14
Tennessee Johnson, 52
Their One Love, 50
They Died With Their Boots On, 53
Turner, Ted, 30
Uncle Tom's Cabin, 2
Undefeated, The, 53
Using Civil War Films, 2-4
Vidor, King, 50
Virginia City, 54
Vogel, Virgil, 20
Wallis, H., 49, 53, 54
Walsh, Raoul, 19, 24, 53
Warren, C.M., 49
Watkins, L., 31
Webb, R., 39
Weinstein, B., 23, 28
Weinstein, H., 23
Weisbart, D., 39
White, Larry, 22
White, S., 48
Wicked Spring, 54

Wolper, D., 41, 42, 48
Wyler, William, 27, 36
Young Mr. Lincoln, 55
Zanuck, D., 55
Zwick, Edward, 29, 37

www.ingramcontent.com/pod-product-compliance
Lightning Source LLC
Chambersburg PA
CBHW021136300426
44113CB00006B/444